# HOW WOMEN TEST MEN

# HOW WOMEN TEST MEN

## Pass Her Hidden Challenges

## DARRIN ELFORD

How Women Test Men: Pass Her Hidden Challenges

Copyright © 2025 by Darrin Elford

First published by Darrin Elford 2025

The information contained within this book is strictly for information and educational purposes only. If you wish to apply the ideas contained in this book, you are taking full responsibility for your actions.

ISBN:    978-1-991363-11-4  (Paperback)

eISBN:   978-1-991363-12-1  (E-Book)

First edition

# Acknowledgements

Writing this book has been a journey filled with insights, growth, and the support of many incredible people. First and foremost, I want to thank the women in my life - past and present - who have inspired me to dive deeper into the dynamics of relationships and how women test men. Your challenges, feedback, tests and wisdom have been invaluable in shaping the ideas I share here.

To my readers: thank you for picking up this book. You're already taking the first step towards becoming a better, more confident man in your relationships. I hope the tools and insights within these pages empower you to understand yourself and the women in your life in a way you never have before. Remember that women test men they are interested in to determine their 'mate value' and masculine strength.

I also want to express my deepest gratitude to my loved ones who helped turn my ideas into a structured, coherent, and readable book. Your hard work and patience have made this possible, and for that, I am truly grateful.

To my mentors: your guidance, support, and encouragement have shaped my career and helped me refine the concepts I teach. Your influence has been a key part of my growth as both a writer and a teacher.

Finally, to the countless men and women who have shared their personal experiences with me over the years, thank you. Your stories and struggles have been the fuel for my understanding of this subject, and I am honored to have learned from each of you.

This book wouldn't have been possible without all of you. Thank you for your wisdom, your trust, and your unwavering support.

# Table of Contents

# Introduction

As men, we often find ourselves in relationships where we sense that something is happening—some kind of test—but we're not sure what it is or how to pass it. We may feel confused, frustrated, or even defensive. Why does she seem to challenge us, push our buttons, or ask questions that feel like we're being judged? The truth is, these "tests" are not about trying to trip you up or create drama. They are a natural part of how women assess a man's strength, character, and suitability for a long-term relationship.

In *How Women Test Men: Pass Her Hidden Challenges*, I'm going to take you behind the curtain and show you exactly why women test men, how to recognize these tests when they happen, and most importantly, how to pass them with confidence, ease, and emotional intelligence.

You see, the tests women give men aren't always obvious. Sometimes they come in the form of subtle comments, changes in behavior, or indirect questions that seem to have no real answer. Other times, they might be more direct, challenging your decisions or questioning your commitment. But in every case, they are opportunities for you to prove your worth—not just to her, but to yourself as well.

The journey in this book will take you from a place of uncertainty, where you may feel like you're walking on eggshells or constantly second-guessing yourself, to a place where you fully understand what she's testing, why she's testing you, and how to respond in a way that strengthens your relationship.

In the first chapter, we'll talk about why women test men in the first place. You'll learn that these tests aren't about tricking you, but about helping her assess whether you have the qualities she's looking for in a partner—things like emotional strength, integrity, leadership, and long-term commitment.

By the second chapter, we'll dive into how you can start to recognize when you're being tested. These tests can happen in conversations, through body language, or even in everyday situations. You'll learn to spot the signs and, most importantly, understand what she's really looking for when she challenges you.

In Chapter 3, we'll take a deep dive into the most common tests women give men. You'll discover what passing or failing each test looks like, so you can approach each situation with clarity and confidence. And in the final chapter, we'll talk about how to become the kind of man who doesn't just pass these tests, but handles them with ease and calm. You'll learn how to develop emotional intelligence, build self-confidence, and lead your relationships with a sense of purpose.

This book isn't just about passing tests—it's about becoming the kind of man who knows himself, who understands his role in a relationship, and who can handle whatever comes his way with strength, integrity, and a clear sense of direction.

If you're ready to stop feeling uncertain about what she's really looking for and start becoming the man who confidently meets those challenges, then this book is for you. Let's get started.

# 1

# The Mystery of Her Tests

## Introducing the Concept of Testing

When you're in a relationship with a woman, it's likely that at some point, you've felt like you were being tested. Maybe she asks a question that seems to have no right answer, or she reacts in a way that leaves you confused. You might wonder, "Why is she testing me? What does she want from me?" It's easy to misunderstand these moments, but the truth is, these "tests" are not about trying to trap you, make you feel small, or challenge your worth. In fact, they are a natural and important part of how women evaluate a man's strength, character, and suitability for a long-term relationship.

### Misunderstanding the Tests

For many men, the idea of being "tested" feels uncomfortable. You might think it's unfair, unnecessary, or even manipulative. It can leave you feeling frustrated or unsure of how to react. But these tests aren't about creating conflict or drama—they are, in fact, a woman's way of assessing whether you possess the qualities she is looking for in a partner.

From a male perspective, it may feel like these tests are random, confusing, or just a way to stir up trouble. But in reality, they are often subtle checks that happen naturally in the course of your interactions. Women may not always even realize they're testing you. It's important to remember that these challenges are not personal attacks. Instead, they are part of how women gauge your masculinity, emotional resilience, and overall compatibility.

## The Purpose of These Tests

So, why do women test men? What is the purpose behind these subtle challenges?

- **Evaluating Masculinity and Strength**:
  One of the core things a woman looks for in a partner is a man who is emotionally strong and able to stand firm when things get tough. Women want to know that you can handle stress, conflict, and difficult situations without falling apart or becoming overly reactive. These tests often come in the form of challenges to see how you handle pressure, disappointment, or adversity.

- **Emotional Intelligence**:
  Women also test men to evaluate their emotional intelligence. Can you understand her feelings? Are you able to respond to her emotions with empathy and patience? Can you communicate openly and calmly, especially when emotions are running high? This ability to understand and manage emotions is key to building a strong, lasting connection.

- **Integrity**:
  A woman wants to know that you have integrity—that you're trustworthy and true to your word. These tests might involve seeing if you'll stick to your promises or how you react in situations where your character is challenged. Do you act with honesty, even when it's difficult? Women will often test this aspect of your personality to make sure they can trust you in the long run.

- **Compatibility**:
  Lastly, many tests revolve around assessing compatibility. This means evaluating whether your values, goals, and lifestyles align. A

woman wants to be sure that you're a good fit for her, not just in terms of attraction, but also in terms of long-term goals and stability. These tests can come in the form of questions about your future, your beliefs, and how you see the relationship developing.

## Why Women Test Men: Evolution and Security

The reason women test men can be traced back to evolutionary instincts and the need for security, stability, and emotional protection.

- **Evolution**:
  From an evolutionary standpoint, women have always sought out partners who could provide not only for their own survival but also for the survival of any future children. In ancient times, this meant choosing men who were strong, reliable, and able to protect and support a family. These traits didn't just involve physical strength—they involved emotional resilience, decision-making skills, and the ability to lead. Tests, then, became a way to determine if a man had these qualities.

- **Security**:
  Women are wired to seek out security, not just physically but emotionally as well. They need to feel safe and secure with the man they are with—both in terms of the relationship and in their day-to-day lives. The tests you face are often ways for her to ensure that you can provide that security. If she feels safe, supported, and understood, she can relax and invest more deeply in the relationship.

- **Emotional Stability**:
  Another reason women test men is to ensure that their partner has emotional stability. Relationships can be intense and challenging, and women want to know that the man they are with won't crumble under pressure. Can he manage his emotions in tough times? Is he able to support her emotionally when things get rough? These tests

help women gauge how well you will handle life's ups and downs together.

- **Seeking Long-Term Partners**:

    Lastly, women test men to determine if they are suitable long-term partners. As women often seek stability, they want to be sure that the man they choose will be a good companion not just for today, but for years to come. Whether it's through tests about commitment, leadership, or emotional resilience, the goal is to make sure that the man they are with has the potential to be a strong, reliable, and loving partner for the long haul.

## Conclusion

Understanding that these tests are not personal or meant to create conflict is crucial. Rather, they are a way for women to assess if a man has the qualities they need in a life partner. These tests help women determine whether you are someone who can provide security, handle challenges, and build a stable, loving relationship.

In the next chapters, we'll dive deeper into the specific tests women give, how to recognize them, and most importantly, how to pass them with calmness and confidence. By understanding these tests and responding with emotional intelligence and strength, you'll not only pass her challenges, but you'll become the kind of man who attracts and maintains a lasting, fulfilling relationship.

## The Hidden Nature of the Tests

When it comes to the tests women give men, one of the most important things to understand is that they're not always obvious. In fact, many of the tests women use aren't even conscious on their part. They're often driven by deep, emotional needs and instincts that women may not be fully aware of. This makes them harder to spot, and more difficult to navigate, if you don't know what to look for.

## Subconscious Behavior Driven by Emotional Needs

You may have noticed that sometimes a woman's behavior seems confusing or unpredictable. One minute she's warm and affectionate, and the next, she seems distant or challenging. This shift can be an indication that she is unconsciously testing you—trying to see how you react to certain emotional situations. These shifts in behavior aren't usually done to manipulate or cause trouble; instead, they stem from her deeper emotional needs and instincts.

For instance, when a woman seems to pull away or give you a "cold shoulder," it may not be because she's upset with you personally. Often, it's a test to see how you handle emotional distance. Is it because you're emotionally strong enough to give her the space she needs without becoming insecure or needy? Or does it cause you to react in a way that makes her feel like you're not emotionally stable?

These tests are often connected to things like her need for reassurance, security, or emotional stability. Women may not always be aware that they are testing you in these moments. It could be that her emotional needs are causing her to act in ways that challenge you, almost without thinking. But the way you respond to these emotional shifts can tell her a lot about your emotional intelligence, strength, and ability to be a supportive partner.

## Misinterpreting Tests as Challenges or Manipulation

One of the biggest mistakes men often make is interpreting these tests as personal challenges or even as manipulative tactics. When a woman seems to test you—whether it's by questioning your intentions, making a subtle remark, or showing frustration—you may feel like you're being attacked or judged. This can lead to confusion, frustration, or even defensive behavior on your part.

For example, if she questions your commitment or asks about your future together, you might interpret this as her doubting your intentions or trying to put pressure on you. It can feel like she's challenging your loyalty or trying to manipulate you into making promises you're not ready for. But in reality, she might simply be testing whether you can handle difficult questions with calmness, honesty, and confidence.

In another case, if she asks you to make a decision or take the lead in a situation, you may feel like she's trying to control you or criticize your ability to lead. But this could be a test to see if you're decisive, confident, and capable of handling responsibility in the relationship. She might be looking for assurance that you can take charge when needed, especially in challenging situations.

When men misinterpret these tests as challenges or manipulative tactics, the result is often defensiveness. You may react by withdrawing, becoming defensive, or even arguing, which only makes the situation more tense and harder to navigate. Women, on the other hand, are often looking for reassurance, emotional strength, or clarity—not for confrontation or power struggles.

## Why This Happens

The reason why these tests can feel like challenges or manipulations is that, as men, we are wired to respond to conflict in ways that are more direct and often more rational. We want to fix problems, solve issues, and move on. So when we feel like we're being tested, we might view it as an attack or a puzzle that needs to be solved immediately.

But relationships don't always work this way. Women are more likely to approach emotional challenges indirectly and emotionally. When they test us, they often want to see if we can meet their emotional needs, not just solve their problems. They want to feel secure, validated, and understood. This means that, instead of reacting defensively, it's more important to respond with patience, empathy, and emotional intelligence.

## Conclusion

Understanding that many of the tests women give are not conscious can help you approach them with a different mindset. Instead of seeing these moments as personal attacks or manipulative games, try to recognize that they are driven by emotional needs and instincts. When you can shift your perspective and respond with emotional strength, calmness, and empathy, you'll not only pass these tests—you'll strengthen the relationship and become the kind of man she can rely on.

In the next chapters, we'll explore how to recognize these hidden tests and, more importantly, how to navigate them with confidence and clarity. Once you start seeing these challenges as opportunities to show your emotional intelligence and stability, you'll find that passing her tests becomes easier and more natural.

## The Impact of Ignorance

When men fail to recognize the tests women give, the consequences can be significant. Without understanding why certain things are happening in the relationship, confusion, conflict, and frustration often follow. In this chapter, we'll explore what happens when men miss these tests, why it leads to misunderstandings, and how it can prevent growth and understanding in the relationship.

## Confusion and Misunderstanding

One of the most common reactions when men fail to recognize these tests is confusion. You might find yourself wondering, *Why is she acting this way?* or *What does she want from me?* This confusion often arises because the tests aren't always obvious. They can be subtle—small comments, changes in behavior, or emotional shifts that seem out of nowhere. When you don't understand that these are actually tests, you may interpret them as random or inexplicable actions.

For example, she might ask you about your plans for the future together, or she might seem distant or withdrawn for no apparent reason. You may start to question if she's upset with you, if she's losing interest, or if something is wrong with the relationship. In truth, these moments are likely not signs of a deeper problem—they're simply tests designed to gauge your emotional strength, commitment, or leadership. But without recognizing them for what they are, you can end up spinning your wheels, trying to figure out what went wrong, when nothing actually has.

## Conflict and Miscommunication

Another result of failing to recognize these tests is conflict. When you don't understand why she's acting a certain way, it's easy to become defensive or frustrated. You might feel attacked or challenged, even though she's not trying to do either. This defensive reaction can lead to miscommunication, as both parties struggle to express themselves and understand each other's intentions.

For example, if she questions your commitment or makes a remark about your relationship, and you respond defensively, it could escalate into an argument. You might feel like she's accusing you of something, and she might feel like you're not taking her concerns seriously. Instead of understanding that she's testing how you handle pressure or emotional topics, you might see it as a confrontation. This can create tension and hurt feelings on both sides.

When these misunderstandings happen repeatedly, they can build into a bigger problem—one that isn't necessarily about the issue at hand but about the lack of communication and emotional awareness. The failure to recognize these tests can lead to constant conflict and frustration, making it difficult for either partner to feel heard or understood.

## Frustration in Relationships

When you don't recognize that you're being tested, frustration sets in—both for you and for her. As a man, you might feel like no matter what you do, you can't seem to get things right. You may try to solve the problem or respond to her needs, but without fully understanding what she's looking for, your efforts can fall short. You may feel like you're walking on eggshells, constantly second-guessing yourself, and unsure of how to respond in a way that satisfies her.

On the other hand, she might feel frustrated as well. If she's testing you to see how emotionally strong or committed you are and you don't rise to the occasion, she might start to doubt your ability to lead the relationship or meet her needs. She might feel disconnected or unsupported, which can lead to further emotional distance. This frustration on both sides can create a sense of growing tension in the relationship, making it harder to build a strong foundation of trust and understanding.

## An Opportunity for Growth and Understanding

What many men fail to realize is that these "tests" are not obstacles or traps - they are opportunities for growth and understanding. Every time you face a test, you have the chance to show emotional intelligence, resilience, and leadership. Instead of seeing these moments as challenges or threats, try to view them as opportunities to deepen your connection with her and learn more about yourself.

For example, when she asks about your long-term intentions or pulls away emotionally, these moments can be a chance for you to reflect on your own feelings and communicate openly. By responding with clarity, confidence, and understanding, you show her that you are emotionally mature and capable of handling difficult conversations. This not only strengthens the relationship but also helps you grow as a person.

The key to passing these tests with ease is awareness. Once you recognize that these moments aren't meant to cause harm, but to help her evaluate your emotional qualities, you can approach them with a calm mindset. Instead of feeling pressured or defensive, you can respond in a way that demonstrates your maturity and understanding.

## Conclusion

Failing to recognize the tests women give can lead to confusion, conflict, and frustration in relationships. But when you see these tests for what they are— opportunities to grow and prove your emotional strength—you'll start to handle them with calmness and confidence. Instead of feeling defeated or misunderstood, you'll find that these moments become opportunities to build a deeper, more connected relationship. In the next chapters, we'll dive into how to recognize these tests when they happen and how to pass them with ease.

# 2

# Recognize When She is Testing You

## Recognizing the Subtle Signs

One of the most challenging aspects of understanding the tests women give men is that these tests often don't look like tests at all. They tend to come in subtle, even confusing forms—small shifts in behavior, indirect comments, or challenges to your values and decisions. This makes them hard to spot, especially if you're not familiar with what to look for. But once you begin to recognize these signs, you'll find that you can respond with greater awareness and emotional intelligence.

In this chapter, we'll explore some of the subtle ways these tests show up, including changes in emotional temperature and indirect comments, and how to interpret these signals as opportunities to demonstrate your emotional stability and maturity.

### Subtle Forms of Testing

Women don't always directly ask questions or make bold statements when testing a man. Instead, they may use more subtle ways to evaluate your emotional resilience, leadership, and values. Here are some common, subtle forms of testing:

1. **Changing Moods**:
    One of the most common ways a woman may test you is through shifts in her mood. You might notice that one moment she's warm

and affectionate, and the next, she seems distant, upset, or withdrawn. This can leave you feeling confused or wondering if you've done something wrong. In reality, this emotional shift could be a test to see how you handle emotional fluctuations. Are you emotionally strong enough to stay calm, even when she's not in the best mood? Can you stay grounded and not react impulsively? She might be testing whether you can offer emotional stability during moments of uncertainty.

2. **Indirect Comments**:

Sometimes, a woman may make a comment that seems offhand or light-hearted, but it's actually a way of gauging your reaction. She might casually ask, "Do you think we're really a good match?" or make a comment like, "I wonder if I can really trust you." These types of comments might seem like small talk, but they are often subtle ways of testing how secure you are in the relationship, how much you value her, or how much emotional resilience you have. Your response is key here. Do you become defensive, or do you calmly address her concerns with confidence? How you respond to these indirect comments can reveal a lot about your emotional intelligence and readiness for a serious relationship.

3. **Challenges to Your Values or Decisions**:

A woman might also test your leadership or decision-making abilities by challenging your values or decisions. This can happen in small ways, like questioning why you did something or asking you to explain your reasoning. For example, if you make a decision for the both of you—whether it's about plans for the weekend or how to handle a conflict—she might challenge it just to see how you defend your choice. This is a test of your confidence and ability to stand by your beliefs. Are you able to calmly explain your choices without getting defensive? Can you lead with integrity, even when your decisions are questioned? The way you handle these challenges will show her whether you have the emotional strength and self-assurance she's looking for.

## Emotional Temperature Shifts: Unpredictable Reactions

One of the clearest ways a woman might test you is through sudden emotional shifts—what can feel like a change in "temperature." These mood swings might seem unpredictable or difficult to understand, but they often signal that she's testing your emotional stability.

1. **Mood Swings**:
   If she goes from being loving and affectionate to distant or upset without an obvious cause, it may feel like you're walking on eggshells. You might be tempted to question whether you've done something wrong or overthink the situation. However, these mood swings often aren't about you specifically—they are a way of testing your emotional steadiness. Women want to see if you can remain calm and composed, even when the emotional atmosphere around you is fluctuating. If you react with frustration or insecurity, it can create tension and make her feel uncertain. But if you stay grounded and respond with patience, you'll show her that you can handle emotional ups and downs without becoming overwhelmed.

2. **Unpredictable Reactions**:
   Sometimes, a woman's reaction might seem out of proportion to the situation at hand. Maybe she gets upset about something small, or she reacts to a situation in a way that feels excessive. These reactions can be a test to see how you handle unexpected emotional responses. Can you stay composed and supportive, or do you become defensive or frustrated? Emotional stability is a key quality that women look for in a partner, especially when navigating difficult or unpredictable emotional terrain. How you react in these moments will determine whether you pass the test.

3. **Testing Boundaries**:

Another form of emotional testing involves pushing boundaries to see how you react. She might do this subtly, such as by asking you to do something you're not comfortable with or testing how far she can push your patience. This can feel like a challenge, but it's often a way for her to assess whether you have healthy boundaries and whether you can stand firm in the face of emotional demands. Women want to see if you can navigate these situations without losing your emotional cool or becoming overly accommodating.

## How to Recognize These Subtle Tests

Recognizing these subtle signs requires a shift in mindset. Instead of reacting with confusion or frustration, try to see these moments as opportunities to show your emotional maturity. The key is to stay calm, grounded, and clear-headed, even when the emotional temperature shifts or when you're faced with an indirect comment or challenge.

When she changes her mood or questions your decisions, take a moment to understand what might be going on beneath the surface. Remember, it's not necessarily about the specific issue at hand; it's about how you handle her emotions and your ability to stay steady. If you react with patience, confidence, and empathy, you'll pass the test with flying colors.

## Conclusion

Women often test men in subtle ways, using changes in mood, indirect comments, and challenges to your decisions or values. These tests are designed to evaluate your emotional strength, stability, and leadership. By learning to recognize these signs, you can approach each situation with calmness and emotional intelligence, demonstrating that you're the kind of man who can handle whatever comes your way with confidence and composure. In the next chapter, we'll dive into the specific tests women give and how to pass them with ease.

---

# The Role of Communication

---

Communication is one of the most important aspects of any relationship, but it's also where many tests from women take place. Unlike direct challenges or confrontations, these tests often happen through the way she communicates with you—through what she says and how she says it. By understanding how women test men through communication, you'll be better equipped to navigate these moments with confidence and clarity.

In this chapter, we'll discuss how women often test through both verbal and non-verbal communication, and how you can learn to recognize and respond appropriately.

## How Women Test Through Communication

Women tend to use communication, whether direct or indirect, to assess different aspects of a man's character. Some of these tests may seem like simple conversations or requests, but they are actually ways of evaluating your emotional intelligence, confidence, and the security you provide in the relationship.

1. **Indirect Questions**:

One common way women test men is through indirect questions. These questions may not come right out and ask what they really want to know, but they can reveal a lot about how you respond under pressure. For example, she might ask, "Where do you see this relationship going?" or "Do you think we're a good match?" These questions may seem innocent, but they are often designed to test your commitment, confidence, or your vision for the future.

In these moments, it's important not to panic or feel cornered. Instead, take a breath and respond honestly and confidently. She's testing how secure you are in the relationship and how well you can articulate your feelings and intentions. A calm and thoughtful answer shows emotional maturity and the ability to lead a relationship.

2. **Requests for Reassurance**:

Another way women test men through communication is by seeking reassurance. This might sound like her saying, "You still care about me, right?" or "You're not going to leave me, are you?" While these requests may seem like signs of insecurity, they are often tests to see if you are committed, emotionally stable, and capable of providing the reassurance she needs.

When faced with these requests, it's important to respond in a way that provides emotional security without becoming defensive. Reassure her with confidence and clarity, but avoid over-explaining or sounding unsure. Your calm, confident response will signal to her that you are secure in the relationship and can handle her emotional needs.

3. **Statements About Expectations**:

Sometimes, women will express their expectations indirectly to see how you react. She might say, "I really want to be with someone who knows what they want," or "I don't want to waste time if things aren't serious." These statements are tests to see how well you can handle her needs and whether you can match her level of emotional investment.

In these situations, it's important to stay grounded. Listen to her expectations carefully and consider how you can meet them. Rather than feeling pressured, use this as an opportunity to communicate your own feelings and intentions clearly. Being able to express your values and your direction in the relationship will show her that you're ready to step up as a strong, committed partner.

## Understanding Non-Verbal Cues

In addition to verbal communication, women also communicate through non-verbal cues—body language, tone of voice, and even eye contact. These cues can be just as revealing as what she says, and often serve as a silent test to gauge how emotionally in tune you are with her. Being aware of these signals can help you respond appropriately in situations where words alone might not give you the full picture.

1. **Body Language**:

    Body language can speak volumes, often conveying emotions and intentions that words don't express. If a woman leans in close while talking to you, it might be a sign that she's engaged and emotionally connected. On the other hand, if she crosses her arms, pulls away, or avoids physical contact, it could be a sign of emotional distance or discomfort. These physical cues are a test to see how you react to changes in her emotional state.

    Pay attention to her body language and try to match her level of comfort. If she seems open and engaged, respond with warmth and attentiveness. If she pulls away or seems distant, give her space and show patience, rather than reacting with frustration or confusion.

This demonstrates that you are in tune with her emotions and can handle different emotional states.

## 2. Tone of Voice:

A woman's tone can provide a lot of information about how she's feeling and what she might be testing. A soft, gentle tone might indicate a desire for reassurance or a request for emotional support, while a sharp or irritated tone could signal frustration or dissatisfaction. Her tone may not always align with the words she says, which is why it's important to pay attention to both.

When you hear a tone that's different from what you expect, try to focus on the underlying emotion rather than the words themselves. Responding with empathy and calmness, rather than reacting to the tone or becoming defensive, will help you handle the test and maintain emotional stability in the relationship.

## 3. Eye Contact:

Eye contact is another powerful tool in communication, and it can serve as a subtle test. If she makes direct eye contact, it may indicate trust, openness, and a desire for connection. However, if she avoids eye contact or looks away frequently, it could be a sign that she's feeling uncertain or testing your reaction to emotional distance.

In these situations, it's important to match her level of eye contact without being overly intense. If she's looking at you with trust, return the gaze with confidence. If she's avoiding eye contact, give her the space she needs, but also show that you're present and attentive when she's ready to reconnect.

## Conclusion

Communication is at the heart of many of the tests women give men. Whether through indirect questions, requests for reassurance, or statements about expectations, women use communication to test your emotional intelligence, commitment, and maturity. Along with verbal communication, non-verbal cues like body language, tone of voice, and eye contact also play a critical role in these tests. By paying close attention to both what is being said and how it's being said, you can respond in a way that demonstrates emotional stability, understanding, and leadership. In the next chapter, we'll dive deeper into specific tests women give and how to pass them with ease and confidence.

## The Context of the Test

When it comes to understanding the tests women give men, it's crucial to recognize that timing and context play significant roles. These tests don't happen randomly. They often arise in moments of emotional tension or when reassurance is needed. Understanding when and why these tests occur will help you respond more effectively, strengthening your connection and building a deeper level of trust.

In this chapter, we'll explore the importance of timing in these tests and how they can emerge at different stages of a relationship—whether you're in the early stages of dating or already in a long-term partnership.

### Why Timing Matters

Timing plays a crucial role in the tests women give men. These tests often come up during moments of emotional tension, uncertainty, or when reassurance is needed. The emotional environment in which these tests occur can make a big difference in how you interpret and respond to them. Here's why timing matters:

1. **Emotional Tension**:

    Many tests happen when there's emotional tension in the relationship. This could be a disagreement, a difficult conversation, or simply a moment when one or both partners are feeling vulnerable. In these situations, a woman may test your emotional stability to see how you handle stress and emotional challenges. She wants to know if you can stay calm and supportive during these tough moments.

    For example, after an argument, she might suddenly ask questions about your future together or make indirect comments to gauge whether you're still committed. These tests aren't about the argument itself, but about seeing how you handle the emotional aftermath. Are you quick to reassure her, or do you become defensive or shut down? Your response to these moments will help her feel secure, or it may leave her feeling uncertain.

2. **Need for Reassurance**:

    Tests can also arise when a woman is feeling insecure or uncertain about the relationship. In these cases, she might use a test to check whether you can provide the reassurance she needs. This could come in the form of a simple question like, "Do you still care about me?" or "Where do you see us going?" When she asks these kinds of questions, the timing may be triggered by an emotional need for affirmation, not necessarily a lack of commitment or trust in you. How you respond—calmly, confidently, and with reassurances—will show her that she has a strong, reliable partner who can provide the emotional support she seeks.

## Situational Tests: Early Dating vs. Long-Term Partnership

Another key factor in understanding the context of these tests is recognizing how they differ depending on the stage of the relationship. Whether you're in the early stages of dating or already in a long-term partnership, the nature of the tests will shift as the relationship grows and evolves.

1. **Early Dating**:

   In the early stages of dating, women often test men to assess whether they are emotionally available, trustworthy, and capable of building a future together. These tests may be more subtle and focused on gauging your intentions. She might ask questions about your past relationships, your goals, or your values to understand if you're a good match.

   For instance, she might ask, "What do you want out of life?" or "How do you feel about commitment?" These are common early-stage tests that reveal your readiness for a serious relationship and your emotional depth. The timing here matters because she is looking for signals that you are serious, stable, and have the qualities needed for a long-term partnership. If you respond confidently and honestly, showing that you are emotionally available and ready to build something meaningful, you'll pass these tests with flying colors.

2. **Long-Term Partnership**:

   As relationships progress and move into long-term partnerships, the tests become more focused on the deeper aspects of emotional stability, leadership, and shared values. These tests are often less about intention and more about character. She may challenge your ability to lead the relationship, handle difficult situations, or provide security and emotional support over time.

For example, after years together, she might test your commitment during times of stress—such as when you're going through a difficult period at work or facing personal challenges. She could test your emotional resilience by questioning your ability to handle tough situations calmly or by pushing you to see how you react when the relationship faces adversity. These tests are about seeing if you have grown and evolved as a partner, and whether you can still provide the strength and stability needed to carry the relationship through life's challenges.

Long-term relationship tests might also involve testing how you balance the needs of the partnership with personal growth and individual goals. She might ask, "Do you still see a future together?" or "How do you think we can continue to grow together?" These are tests of both emotional connection and the ability to evolve as partners, not just individuals.

## Recognizing the Patterns of Testing

Whether the relationship is in its early stages or well into the long term, the key to recognizing these tests is understanding the underlying purpose behind them. These tests are not meant to trap you or create conflict, but rather to evaluate your emotional maturity, stability, and commitment.

Each stage of the relationship comes with its own set of challenges, and the tests will reflect that. In the early dating phase, women are looking to see if you're capable of a serious relationship. In long-term partnerships, the focus shifts to emotional resilience, leadership, and the ability to handle life's ups and downs together. By understanding these stages, you can respond more effectively and be the kind of partner who can meet her emotional needs at every phase of the relationship.

## Conclusion

The context of the test—whether it's during a moment of emotional tension, a need for reassurance, or in different stages of the relationship—matters more than you might realize. Timing is critical in understanding the nature of these tests. Early on, they are about assessing compatibility and emotional availability, while in long-term relationships, they shift towards testing stability, growth, and commitment. By recognizing the context of the test, you can respond with calmness, understanding, and confidence, proving that you are the steady and reliable partner she's seeking.

# 3

## Major Tests Women Give Men

### Emotional Stability Tests

One of the most important tests women give men is the **Emotional Stability Test**. This test is all about how you handle stress, pressure, and challenging situations. Life isn't always smooth sailing, and relationships will inevitably face bumps along the way. During these times, a woman wants to see how emotionally steady you are. Can you stay calm when things go wrong? Or do you react in a way that creates more chaos or tension?

In this chapter, we'll explore some common emotional stability tests, what it looks like to pass them, and how failing them can harm your relationship.

### Examples of Emotional Stability Tests

1. **"How do you handle stress?"**

   Stress is a natural part of life—whether it's work pressure, personal challenges, or external situations. When a woman asks, "How do you handle stress?" or brings up something related to stress, she's testing to see how you react when you're under pressure.

   She's wondering if you can stay calm and composed when life feels overwhelming, or if you crumble and react impulsively. This test might not always come in the form of a direct question; sometimes, it's about how you respond when something stressful happens in the relationship or in your personal life. For example, when you have a bad day at work or face a difficult situation, how you react will give her a clear picture of your emotional resilience.

2. **"How do you react when things go wrong?"**

Life throws curveballs at everyone. Whether it's a sudden change in plans, a disagreement, or an unexpected setback, things are bound to go wrong. When she tests your reaction to these situations, she wants to see if you can handle challenges without letting them overwhelm you.

If you keep your cool, stay solution-oriented, and remain positive despite the setback, you show her that you're someone who can be relied upon in tough times. But if you overreact—whether by becoming defensive, angry, or withdrawing—she'll likely feel that you don't have the emotional maturity to handle pressure effectively.

### Passing the Emotional Stability Test

To pass this test, you need to demonstrate that you can handle stress and challenges with grace. Here's what a pass looks like:

1. **Remaining Calm and Composed:**

When something stressful happens, you maintain your composure. You don't let your emotions take over or react impulsively. Instead, you stay level-headed and assess the situation before responding. This shows that you're in control of your emotions, not the other way around.

2. **Solution-Oriented Thinking**:

Emotional stability is also about finding solutions rather than focusing on the problem. If things go wrong, do you immediately look for ways to fix it? Or do you become paralyzed by frustration or fear? When you respond by thinking through solutions, even in difficult moments, it shows that you're able to navigate challenges with a clear mind.

3. **Empathy and Support**:

In tough situations, it's important to not only handle your own emotions but also support your partner. If she is upset or stressed, you should be able to provide comfort, reassurance, and a listening ear. Your ability to offer emotional support in difficult times speaks volumes about your emotional intelligence and stability.

4. **Patience**:

Emotional stability requires patience, especially when things don't go as planned. Rather than rushing into a reaction, you take a step back, breathe, and choose a measured response. This shows that you're not easily rattled and can maintain peace even when life is chaotic.

### Failing the Emotional Stability Test

On the other hand, failing this test usually happens when you allow your emotions to control your behavior. Here's what a fail looks like:

1. **Becoming Defensive**:

When faced with stress or criticism, you become defensive, trying to protect yourself instead of focusing on the situation. For example, if something goes wrong and she asks how you'll handle it, you might respond with irritation or a dismissive attitude instead of showing a desire to solve the issue. This is a clear sign that you lack emotional control and are unable to take responsibility for challenges.

2. **Getting Angry or Irritable**:

   If you react with anger or frustration when things don't go as planned, this shows a lack of emotional maturity. For instance, if you're dealing with a problem at work and your frustration spills over into the relationship, it might make her feel unsafe or unsupported. An angry response signals that you aren't able to manage your emotions and that stress is getting the best of you.

3. **Withdrawing or Shutting Down**:

   Another way men fail this test is by withdrawing emotionally when things go wrong. Instead of staying engaged and working through the problem, you may shut down, become distant, or refuse to talk about what's bothering you. This can leave her feeling disconnected and unsure of where you stand in the relationship. Emotional withdrawal can create unnecessary tension and make it difficult to resolve issues in a healthy way.

4. **Overreacting**:

   If you overreact to a situation—whether it's by yelling, storming off, or spiralling into panic—she'll quickly see that you're not emotionally steady. Overreaction can create fear or insecurity, especially if the situation didn't warrant such a response. This shows that you're not able to maintain emotional balance in tough situations, which can erode trust and stability in the relationship.

## Why Emotional Stability Matters

The way you handle stress and emotional challenges plays a huge role in the overall health of the relationship. Women are looking for a man who can handle life's ups and downs with grace, someone who can remain steady in the face of difficulty. Emotional stability provides a sense of security, and when she knows you can manage pressure without falling apart, it builds confidence in your ability to be a supportive and dependable partner.

Remember, it's not about being perfect or never feeling stressed. Everyone faces emotional challenges, but how you react in those moments is what matters most. By staying calm, focused, and empathetic, you show that you are the kind of man who can be trusted to handle life's toughest moments with strength and composure.

## Conclusion

Emotional stability tests are an essential part of the relationship-building process. How you handle stress, setbacks, and pressure reveals a lot about your emotional maturity. Passing these tests involves staying calm, composed, and solution-focused, while failing them often involves reacting defensively, angrily, or withdrawing. By practicing emotional control and resilience, you can build a strong foundation of trust and security in your relationship, showing that you are the reliable and steady partner she's looking for.

## Commitment Tests

One of the most significant tests women give men in a relationship is the **Commitment Test**. These tests are designed to evaluate how serious you are about the relationship, your intentions for the future, and whether you're truly invested in building something long-term together. Commitment is a cornerstone of any successful relationship, and women want to be sure that the man they're with is on the same page about where things are headed.

In this chapter, we'll dive into what commitment tests look like, how you can pass them with confidence, and what happens if you fail them.

### Examples of Commitment Tests

1. **"Where do you see this relationship going?"**

   One of the most direct ways a woman will test your commitment is by asking, "Where do you see this relationship going?" She's looking for clarity on whether you're thinking long-term or if you're just going with the flow without any real direction. This question often comes when she's feeling unsure about the future of the relationship or when she wants to know if you share the same goals.

2. **"How serious are you about us?"**

   Another common commitment test is when she asks, "How serious are you about us?" or something similar. This is an indication that she's seeking reassurance that you're as invested in the relationship as she is. She wants to know if you're thinking about taking the relationship to the next level—whether that's exclusivity, moving in together, or planning a future. The question is meant to gauge your level of dedication to the relationship and your willingness to make it a priority.

3. **"What do you want from this relationship?"**

   Sometimes the question might be framed differently, like "What do you want from this relationship?" or "What are you looking for in a partner?" In these moments, she's testing whether you have a clear vision of the relationship and if you see a future together. She wants to know that you're not just casually dating but that you're intentional about where things are headed.

## Passing the Commitment Test

To pass these commitment tests, the key is to show her that you have a clear vision for the future and that you are serious about building a lasting relationship. Here's what passing this test looks like:

1. **Expressing Clarity and Sincerity**:

    When she asks about the future of the relationship, be clear and sincere about your intentions. Don't beat around the bush or offer vague responses. A straightforward, honest answer will go a long way in showing that you're on the same page. For example, if she asks, "Where do you see this relationship going?" you could respond with something like, "I see us building a strong future together, moving forward with trust and commitment. I value what we have and can definitely see us growing as partners."

2. **Being Honest About Your Feelings**:

    It's important to be honest about how you feel and where you stand. If you are ready for a long-term relationship, express that with confidence. If you're not quite sure yet, it's better to say that honestly than to pretend to have all the answers. Women appreciate honesty, even if it means taking a bit more time to figure things out. However, if you're not serious about the relationship, this is also the time to be clear and not lead her on.

3. **Reaffirming Your Commitment:**

Commitment tests are often designed to gauge whether you're truly invested. By reaffirming your commitment to the relationship and talking about your future plans together, you show that you are reliable and serious. Reassurance is essential in these moments, so don't hesitate to express how much she means to you and that you see a future with her.

4. **Talking About Long-Term Goals:**

If you truly are thinking long-term, bring up your shared goals for the future. Discuss how you want to grow together, whether that's through supporting each other's personal aspirations, building a home, or starting a family. When you show that you are aligned in your visions, it proves that you are committed to building something meaningful.

### Failing the Commitment Test

Failing a commitment test usually happens when you avoid the conversation or give vague, non-committal answers. Here's what a fail looks like:

1. **Avoiding the Conversation:**

One of the biggest red flags for women is when a man avoids the commitment conversation altogether. If she asks where you see the relationship going, and you brush it off or change the subject, it sends a message that you're not ready to talk about the future or that you're not invested. Avoiding these conversations can leave her feeling insecure and uncertain about where she stands with you.

## 2. Offering Vague, Non-Committal Responses:

Another way to fail the commitment test is by giving a vague, unclear response. Saying something like, "I don't know what's going to happen" or "Let's just see how things go" can make her feel as though you're not thinking seriously about the future. While it's okay not to have all the answers, offering a clear indication of your intentions or at least a willingness to talk about it is essential. Non-committal responses make it seem like you're not fully invested, and that can lead to doubts and insecurity in the relationship.

## 3. Expressing Doubts or Hesitations:

If you express doubts or hesitations about the relationship when she asks, it can make her question your feelings. Statements like, "I'm not sure if I'm ready for anything serious" or "I'm just not thinking that far ahead" can create doubt and insecurity. While it's important to be honest, consistently expressing hesitation without a clear vision can make her feel uncertain and unsure of your level of commitment.

## 4. Leading Her On:

Another way men fail commitment tests is by leading a woman on. This happens when you act as though you're serious about the relationship but are not fully invested in the long-term future. If you say all the right things but your actions don't align with those words (like avoiding discussions about the future or not following through on promises), she'll begin to feel like you're not truly committed, even if you're giving her hope.

## Why Commitment Tests Are Important

Commitment tests are crucial because they reveal whether you're truly serious about building a future together. They're not meant to trap you or manipulate you—they are opportunities to show your partner that you have a clear vision for the relationship and that you're ready to take things to the next level. Women want to feel secure in knowing that their partner is just as committed to the relationship as they are.

Responding with clarity, honesty, and reassurance helps build trust and creates a sense of emotional security. By passing these tests, you show that you are dependable, reliable, and ready to invest in the future of the relationship.

## Conclusion

Commitment tests are a normal part of any relationship, especially when the relationship begins to get more serious. Women want to know that the man they're with is equally invested in their future together. By expressing clarity about your intentions, being honest, and reassuring her about your long-term plans, you demonstrate that you're committed and ready for the next step. On the other hand, avoiding the conversation or offering vague responses only creates doubt and confusion. Pass these tests with sincerity, and you'll strengthen your relationship for the long haul.

## Strength and Leadership Tests

In any relationship, one of the most important qualities women look for in a man is **strength**—both emotional and mental—and the ability to lead. Women often give subtle yet powerful **Strength and Leadership Tests** to gauge how capable you are in making decisions, providing guidance, and taking responsibility. These tests are about how well you handle challenges, whether you can take charge in difficult situations, and if you have a clear sense of direction in your life.

In this section, we'll look at some common strength and leadership tests, how to pass them with confidence, and what can happen if you fail them.

## Examples of Strength and Leadership Tests

1. **"Do you know what you want in life?"**

   This is one of the most direct ways a woman will test your strength and leadership abilities. When she asks, "Do you know what you want in life?" she's trying to determine whether you have a clear vision for your future. She wants to see if you have direction, purpose, and goals, both for your personal life and your relationship. This question isn't about having all the answers but about showing that you're actively working toward something and have a sense of where you're going.

2. **"What would you do if something happened to me?"**
   This test often comes when there's emotional tension or a situation that causes her to feel vulnerable. She wants to see if you can step up as a protector and leader in difficult times. Asking, "What would you do if something happened to me?" is a way for her to check how you'd respond if things got serious, like if she were hurt or in trouble. This test is not just about your actions in an emergency, but about whether you can be counted on to provide security, guidance, and support.

3. **"How would you handle a tough situation?"**

Women often test a man's leadership ability by presenting hypothetical tough situations, such as dealing with a personal crisis or making a difficult decision. For example, she might ask, "How would you handle a situation where we have financial problems or have to move for work?" She wants to know that you're capable of handling problems with strength and that you can make decisions under pressure.

### Passing the Strength and Leadership Test

Passing strength and leadership tests requires showing that you are **decisive, confident, and have a sense of direction in your life**. Here's what passing this test looks like:

1. **Showing Decisiveness**:

    When you're asked tough questions like, "What do you want in life?" or "What would you do if something happened to me?", it's important to answer with confidence and clarity. A decisive answer shows that you're not indecisive or unsure about your future. For instance, if she asks about your goals, you should have an idea of where you want to go and how you plan to get there. Whether it's your career, personal growth, or relationships, showing that you're actively working toward something tells her you have direction.

2. **Demonstrating Confidence**:

    Confidence is a key component of leadership. When you're faced with a leadership test, you need to show that you believe in your ability to make the right decisions and lead by example. For example, if she asks what you'd do in a difficult situation, don't hesitate or second-guess yourself. Show that you are able to think on your feet, make decisions confidently, and take responsibility for the outcome.

3. **Providing Reassurance**:

When a woman asks, "What would you do if something happened to me?" she's seeking reassurance that you'll be strong enough to handle tough situations. This is your chance to show her that you'll step up, provide stability, and protect her. Whether it's dealing with a personal crisis, financial problems, or an emotional challenge, showing that you can remain calm and steady in difficult times is key to passing this test.

4. **Having a Clear Vision for the Future**:

Women want to know that the man they're with has a clear vision for where he's going. If she asks about your plans for the future, she wants to see that you're not just drifting along but actively working toward meaningful goals. Share your goals for your career, your personal growth, and the relationship. Being able to articulate your future plans with confidence shows that you're serious about life and can lead with purpose.

### Failing the Strength and Leadership Test

Failing the strength and leadership test usually happens when you appear indecisive, unsure, or passive. Here's what a fail looks like:

1. **Appearing Indecisive**:

If you struggle to answer when she asks, "What do you want in life?" or "Where do you see yourself in five years?" it can signal that you're unsure about your own direction. Indecision is a major red flag, as it suggests that you might lack the clarity and focus needed to lead a relationship or provide stability. If your responses are filled with uncertainty or hesitation, she might feel that you're not someone she can rely on to make important decisions.

2. **Offering Vague Responses:**

If you avoid being clear about your future plans or offer vague responses like, "I'm not really sure yet" or "I'll figure it out when the time comes," you fail to show leadership. Vague answers convey that you don't have a plan, which can be unsettling for her. She may begin to question whether you have the strength and leadership qualities necessary to support her and the relationship long-term.

3. **Being Passive in Tough Situations:**

When she asks how you would handle a tough situation, such as an emergency or a financial crisis, a passive or unsure response will fail the test. For example, saying, "I don't know, I guess we would just figure it out" lacks leadership and decisiveness. It's important to show that you're capable of taking charge, making decisions, and offering a clear plan of action in difficult times.

4. **Failing to Reassure Her:**

If she asks, "What would you do if something happened to me?" and you respond with something like, "I don't know, I'd probably just panic," it sends a message that you're not someone who can be relied upon in times of crisis. Women need to feel that their partner is a rock they can lean on in tough times. If you fail to provide reassurance or show that you can handle challenging situations, it will shake her confidence in your ability to lead.

## Why Strength and Leadership Tests Are Important

These tests are essential because they show how well you can handle life's challenges and whether you have the strength to lead when needed. Women want a man who is confident, decisive, and capable of taking charge when necessary. Leadership doesn't mean controlling every aspect of the relationship, but it does mean being someone she can rely on to make decisions, provide stability, and take responsibility when things get difficult.

Passing these tests builds trust, security, and respect in the relationship. It shows her that you are strong, reliable, and able to lead both in everyday life and in times of crisis.

## Conclusion

Strength and leadership tests are a natural part of any serious relationship. Women want to know that the man they are with can take charge, make decisions, and provide emotional and physical security. By showing confidence, decisiveness, and a clear vision for the future, you pass these tests and demonstrate your ability to lead with strength. Failing these tests—whether through indecision, passivity, or lack of direction—can create doubt and insecurity in the relationship. By rising to the challenge, you show that you are the kind of partner she can rely on to lead with integrity and confidence.

# Alpha Male/Protective Tests

One of the most instinctual and important tests women give men revolves around the concept of **protection**—both physically and emotionally. These are the **Alpha Male/Protective Tests**, where women look for signs that you can protect them, stand up for them, and lead with strength in difficult or challenging situations. This type of test is meant to assess how you react when their safety or dignity is at stake and whether you can step into a leadership role to ensure they feel secure and valued.

In this chapter, we'll explore the nature of these tests, how to pass them with grace, and what happens when you fail.

## Examples of Alpha Male / Protective Tests

1. **"What would you do if someone disrespects me?"**
   This is a classic example of a protective test. When a woman asks this question, she's looking for your response to a potential threat or situation where her dignity might be challenged. She wants to know how you would react if someone disrespects her in public or behind closed doors. She isn't asking you to go on the offensive immediately, but she wants to see if you're willing to step in and defend her if the situation calls for it.

2. **"How would you protect me?"**

   This is another version of the protective test. It's often phrased when there's a sense of vulnerability, either emotionally or physically. She might ask, "How would you protect me?" as a way of gauging whether you have a natural instinct to care for and shield her from harm. This question often comes when she's feeling insecure or worried, and she wants to know if you have the strength and presence to make her feel safe in any situation.

3. **"What would you do if something happened to me?"**
   This can be framed in many ways, but the underlying purpose is to determine if you are ready and capable of stepping up as a protector. Women often ask this to assess whether you can take charge when

they need support or safety. She's wondering if you will take control of the situation and handle things decisively if the need arises.

## Passing the Alpha Male / Protective Test

To pass these tests, you need to show that you have natural **leadership** and **protective instincts** without coming across as controlling or overbearing. Here's what passing this test looks like:

1. **Demonstrating Leadership and Calm Assurance**

   When a woman asks, "What would you do if someone disrespects me?" she's looking for a calm yet confident answer. The key is not to overreact but to demonstrate that you would handle the situation appropriately. You might say something like, "I would stand up for you, make sure you feel respected, and handle things with calm and confidence. If necessary, I would remove you from the situation to protect your peace." This shows that you have the strength and foresight to protect her without escalating things unnecessarily.

2. **Demonstrating Emotional Strength and Protection**

   Protecting someone isn't just about physical safety—it's also about providing emotional security. If she asks, "How would you protect me?" you can demonstrate emotional protection by showing that you will stand by her during difficult times, protect her from emotional harm, and help create a safe, supportive environment. You can reassure her by saying, "I will always be here to support you, keep our communication open, and make sure you feel valued and respected in all situations."

## 3. Staying Calm in Moments of Challenge

The key to passing any Alpha Male/Protective Test is to show that you can handle challenges calmly and with control. For example, if there is a tense moment, your ability to stay composed, make decisions, and step up to protect her shows leadership. When she sees that you won't panic in difficult situations, it reassures her that she's with a man who can be trusted to provide protection - emotionally, mentally, and physically—if the need arises.

## 4. Setting Healthy Boundaries

Being protective doesn't mean controlling or dominating the situation. It's about being responsible and making sure her best interests are at heart. If someone is disrespecting her, it's important to address it appropriately. This means standing up for her but also knowing when to step back and let her handle things if she prefers. It's about empowering her while ensuring that you're always there to offer protection when necessary.

### Failing the Alpha Male / Protective Test

Failing this test typically happens when you show signs of **passivity, insecurity, or fail to step up** in moments when protection is needed. Here's what failure looks like:

## 1. Being Passive or Indifferent

If a woman asks, "What would you do if someone disrespects me?" and you respond with, "I don't know, I guess I'd let it slide," it shows that you're not willing to stand up for her. Women need a man who will step in and protect them when necessary. Being passive in this situation shows that you aren't confident in your ability to take charge, and it can make her feel unsupported.

2. **Showing Insecurity or Overcompensation**

On the other hand, being overly aggressive in your response can also be a failure. If you say, "I'd beat anyone who disrespects you!" or "I'd confront them right away," it may come across as overcompensating for a lack of true strength. Women want protection, not violence or drama. The key is to show confidence in your ability to handle situations with calm strength, not by overreacting or being aggressive.

3. **Not Stepping Up When Needed**

If a woman is in a vulnerable situation, whether it's an emotional breakdown or dealing with a difficult person, and you fail to step in and offer support, it can be a major failure. Not taking charge when she needs you shows that you lack the protective instincts she's looking for. For example, if she's upset and you ignore her need for comfort, or if there's a situation where she's being disrespected and you don't do anything to help, it will shake her confidence in your ability to be a protector in the relationship.

4. **Lack of Emotional Protection**

Protection isn't just physical; it's also about emotional security. If she feels vulnerable and you don't provide reassurance, or if you dismiss her feelings when she's upset, it fails the protective test. Women need a man who can shield them emotionally from hurt, disrespect, and negativity, not someone who dismisses or invalidates their emotions.

## Why Alpha Male / Protective Tests Are Important

These tests are incredibly important because they highlight the role of a man as a protector and leader. Women are naturally drawn to men who can take charge in tough situations, offer safety, and provide emotional stability. When you show that you are capable of protecting her both physically and emotionally, you build trust and deepen the connection between you.

Women need to feel secure with their partner. These tests allow them to assess whether you have the qualities of an alpha male who is strong, confident, and reliable in times of need. It's not about dominating or controlling, but about being the kind of man who can provide security and calm when things get tough.

## Conclusion

Alpha Male/Protective Tests are essential to understanding a woman's need for security in a relationship. By responding with calm, confidence, and strength, you show that you can be the protector she needs. Failing these tests by being passive, insecure, or unwilling to step up leaves her feeling unsupported and unsafe. Pass these tests, and you will demonstrate your ability to be a dependable, strong partner who can protect and lead with respect and care.

## Value and Integrity Tests

One of the most crucial tests women give men revolves around **value and integrity**—two qualities that are foundational for trust, respect, and long-term commitment. These **Value and Integrity Tests** are meant to assess whether you will stand by your beliefs, morals, and principles, especially when there's pressure to act differently or when you think no one is watching. A woman wants to know that the man she's with will always do the right thing, even when it's difficult, inconvenient, or when there's no one to impress.

In this section, we'll explore the nature of these tests, how to pass them by staying true to your values, and what happens if you fail them.

### Examples of Value and Integrity Tests

1. **"Would you lie for me?"**

   This is one of the more direct tests when it comes to assessing your integrity. A woman might ask, "Would you lie for me?" or "Can I trust you to cover for me?" She's testing whether you're willing to compromise your morals to protect her or avoid conflict. This could come in situations where she might have made a mistake or wants you to support her decision, even if it goes against your personal values.

2. **"What would you do if no one were watching?"**

   Another common question is, "What would you do if no one were watching?" This is designed to test your honesty and moral compass. She wants to see if you would do the right thing, even when there's no external pressure or need to impress anyone. It could be a situation where you're tempted to cut corners or act in a way that might not align with your true values, but there's no one around to see it. Her test is about whether you can be trusted when no one is looking.

3. **"How would you handle a situation where you could get away with something wrong?"**

This might be a subtle test, but it can reveal a lot about your character. For example, she may ask, "What would you do if you were in a situation where it would be easy to cheat or lie, but no one would find out?" The question isn't necessarily about the specific act, but about your moral decision-making process when faced with temptations or opportunities to act against your values.

## Passing the Value and Integrity Test

Passing the Value and Integrity Test requires being **consistent** in your beliefs and actions. It's about demonstrating that you will not compromise your principles, even when the stakes are high or when you think no one is watching. Here's what passing this test looks like:

1. **Aligning with Your Values and Morals**

   The key to passing these tests is to show that you consistently act in alignment with your values, no matter the situation. If she asks, "Would you lie for me?" respond with honesty. You might say, "I would support you in any situation, but I wouldn't lie for you. I believe in honesty and transparency, and I'd want to help you in a way that's aligned with our values." This kind of response shows that you are reliable and morally grounded.

2. **Staying Honest and Transparent**

   If she asks, "What would you do if no one were watching?" you should answer truthfully, showing that you'll always do what's right, whether or not anyone notices. A good response might be, "I'd do what I believe is right, even if there was no reward or recognition. Integrity is important to me, and I would never act in a way that goes against my beliefs, no matter the situation." By giving this type of answer, you show that your values remain constant and that you can be trusted.

3.  **Choosing Integrity Over Convenience**

When faced with situations where it's tempting to take shortcuts, cheat, or lie, the best way to pass is by choosing to do the right thing. For example, if she asks, "What would you do if you could get away with something wrong?" your response should reflect your commitment to integrity, even when there are no consequences. You could say, "I would always do what I believe is right, even if there were no one around to see. My integrity is something I value, and I wouldn't act in a way that goes against my principles, no matter the temptation."

4.  **Maintaining Consistency**

Your actions should match your words. It's not enough to say you value honesty and integrity—your actions need to reflect that. Women will observe how you handle real-life situations, especially when faced with ethical dilemmas. If your behavior aligns with your stated values, it shows her that you're trustworthy and that you lead with integrity.

### Failing the Value and Integrity Test

Failing this test often happens when you **compromise your morals**, act inconsistently, or give in to pressure. Here's what failure looks like:

1.  **Giving In to Pressure**

If you're asked, "Would you lie for me?" and your answer is, "Well, if it really matters to you, I might," it shows that you're willing to sacrifice your values to please her. While it's natural to want to support someone, compromising your integrity in any situation can cause serious damage to trust. Women want to feel confident that the man they're with will always do the right thing, regardless of the situation.

## 2. Showing Inconsistency in Your Values

If your actions don't align with your words, it can be a major red flag. For example, you might say that you value honesty, but when faced with a situation where telling the truth would be uncomfortable or inconvenient, you choose to lie. If your behavior contradicts your stated values, she may feel that you're not reliable or that your integrity is situational.

## 3. Lying or Hiding the Truth

If you lie to protect yourself or avoid conflict, even when she asks directly, "What would you do if no one were watching?" and you give a dishonest answer, you fail the test. Lying undermines trust and shows that you may be willing to compromise your character to avoid consequences. This erodes the foundation of a strong, healthy relationship.

## 4. Being Inconsistent in Decision-Making

If, when faced with a situation where your integrity is tested—such as a moral dilemma or ethical challenge—you make a decision that goes against your values just to avoid discomfort, you fail the test. This shows her that you cannot be counted on to consistently make the right decisions, which can lead to distrust and uncertainty in the relationship.

### Why Value and Integrity Tests Are Important

Value and integrity tests are crucial because they help women assess whether a man can be trusted to build a solid, long-term relationship based on mutual respect, honesty, and commitment. Integrity is the foundation of any meaningful connection, and without it, a relationship is built on shaky ground. These tests ensure that you're not just saying the right things, but that you consistently demonstrate honesty, reliability, and ethical decision-making.

Women want a man who stands by his principles and can be trusted to do the right thing, even when it's difficult or uncomfortable. Passing these tests builds trust and shows that you are a man of character, someone she can rely on in any situation.

---

### Conclusion

Value and Integrity Tests are a natural part of any relationship. Women want to know that the man they are with will always be truthful, consistent, and trustworthy. By standing firm in your values and acting with integrity, you demonstrate that you are a man of character and reliability. Failing these tests by compromising your morals, lying, or showing inconsistency can undermine trust and create doubt in the relationship. Pass these tests, and you show that you are someone who can be trusted to uphold your values and build a solid foundation for the future.

---

## Independence and Space Tests

---

One of the most important elements of any healthy relationship is the ability to maintain **individuality** and **independence**. Women often test how well you respect their need for space and autonomy without feeling threatened by it. These **Independence and Space Tests** are designed to see if you're comfortable with her having her own life, interests, and personal time apart from you, while still feeling secure in your relationship.

In this chapter, we'll explore the nature of these tests, how to pass them by respecting her independence, and what happens when you fail them.

## Examples of Independence and Space Tests

1. **"How would you feel if I need some space?"**

   This is a direct way for a woman to test how you handle her need for personal time or distance. She may ask this question if she feels like she needs to take a break or spend time with friends, pursue her own hobbies, or focus on her career. It's not a reflection of how she feels about the relationship, but rather a check to see if you can handle her wanting some time away without feeling insecure or neglected.

2. **"Are you okay with me having my own life?"**

   This test is similar but broader. Women want to know if you are okay with them maintaining their own hobbies, friendships, and passions outside of the relationship. It's an important question because it shows whether you respect her individuality and her right to have a fulfilling life that doesn't revolve solely around the relationship.

3. **"What if I want to go on a trip without you?"**

   Another form of this test is when she asks about doing something independently, like traveling without you. She may want to see how you react to the idea of her spending time away from you. The goal is to assess whether you trust her and can handle the fact that she has a life outside of the relationship.

## Passing the Independence and Space Test

To pass these tests, you need to show that you respect her **autonomy** while demonstrating your **commitment** and **support**. Here's what passing this test looks like:

1. **Respecting Her Need for Space**

   If she asks, "How would you feel if I need some space?" the key is to respond with understanding and maturity. You could say, "I totally understand that you need your own time. I respect that and support it. I'm happy when you're happy and taking time for yourself is important." This response shows that you're not insecure or threatened by her need for independence. You're confident in yourself and the relationship.

2. **Demonstrating Trust and Security**

   When asked, "Are you okay with me having my own life?" the best way to respond is by showing that you trust her. A good answer could be, "Absolutely. I want you to have your own passions, friendships, and goals. I believe that both of us having our own lives makes the relationship stronger. It's important to me that we both feel fulfilled individually." This response reflects maturity and a healthy balance between togetherness and personal growth.

3. **Being Supportive, Not Controlling**

If she wants to go on a trip without you, rather than feeling possessive or insecure, a positive response would be: "That sounds like a great opportunity for you. I'm sure you'll have a wonderful time, and I'm excited to hear all about it when you get back. I trust you completely." This demonstrates that you are secure in your relationship and fully support her need to explore her own interests, without needing to be involved in everything she does.

4. **Offering Space Without Withholding Love or Support**

Passing this test isn't just about giving her space and leaving her alone. It's about offering her the space she needs while still being emotionally available and supportive. You can give her space to grow and pursue her passions while still providing love, care, and reassurance that you are there for her when she needs you.

### Failing the Independence and Space Test

Failing this test often happens when you exhibit **clinginess**, **jealousy**, or **insecurity** in response to her need for space. Here's what failure looks like:

1. **Showing Clinginess or Over-Dependence**

If she asks for space and you respond by saying something like, "I don't know if I'm okay with that. I feel like you're pulling away from me," it signals that you're overly dependent on her for emotional validation. Clinginess makes her feel suffocated and doesn't allow for the healthy independence that a relationship needs. This is a clear sign that you're struggling with your own insecurity and haven't learned to manage it yet.

## 2. Expressing Jealousy or Possessiveness

When she wants to go on a trip without you or spend time with friends, and you react with jealousy or possessiveness by saying things like, "Why can't I come with you?" or "You're going to leave me behind?" you fail the test. This type of behavior signals that you're insecure and unable to trust her to have her own life outside of the relationship. Women need a partner who is secure enough to allow them to live their lives independently without feeling threatened.

## 3. Withholding Love or Support

If she wants space and you respond by withdrawing affection or being emotionally distant, it shows that you're not capable of handling the balance of giving her space while still offering love and support. For example, if you say, "Fine, I'll give you space, but don't expect me to talk to you or be affectionate," you are punishing her for wanting time for herself. This type of behavior shows emotional immaturity and a lack of understanding of what a healthy relationship looks like.

## 4. Making Her Feel Guilty

Another failure happens when you make her feel guilty for needing space. You might say, "I can't believe you need space. Does this mean you don't care about me?" or "Why can't you just spend more time with me?" This approach puts undue pressure on her and makes her feel like she has to choose between you and her own needs, which is unhealthy and counterproductive.

## Why Independence and Space Tests Are Important

These tests are crucial for understanding the balance between togetherness and individual autonomy in a relationship. Women need to feel that they can have their own life, pursue their passions, and maintain their friendships without being judged or controlled. At the same time, they want to know that their partner is secure enough in the relationship to support them while still nurturing a strong, independent identity.

These tests help women assess whether you have the emotional maturity to handle the ebb and flow of intimacy and independence, which is essential for a lasting relationship. A healthy relationship allows both partners to grow as individuals, while still being emotionally connected and supportive.

## Conclusion

Independence and Space Tests are designed to evaluate how well you respect a woman's autonomy while still offering love and support. To pass these tests, you must demonstrate trust, maturity, and emotional stability, allowing her the freedom to have her own life without feeling insecure or threatened. Failing these tests by being clingy, jealous, or possessive can create tension and insecurity in the relationship. Pass these tests, and you show that you understand the importance of maintaining balance in a healthy, long-lasting partnership.

*4*

# Pass Her Tests with Ease

## Emotional Mastery

In any relationship, your ability to **manage your emotions** is essential, especially when faced with the tests women give men. These tests are often designed to assess how you handle pressure, stress, and emotional challenges. When you are in a situation where your emotional stability is being tested, how you respond can make all the difference in maintaining a strong and healthy relationship. This chapter will focus on **emotional mastery**—how to control your emotional responses during these tests, why self-awareness is crucial, and practical exercises you can use to stay calm and composed in tense moments.

### Controlling Your Emotional Responses to Tests

When faced with tests, it's easy to react impulsively—especially when the emotions involved feel intense or overwhelming. However, emotional reactions such as anger, frustration, or defensiveness often cloud your judgment and can harm the relationship. **Emotional mastery** means learning to **pause**, assess the situation, and choose a response that reflects maturity, composure, and wisdom.

## Here's how to control your emotional responses:

1. **Pause Before Reacting**

   One of the most important tools you have in emotional mastery is the ability to pause. When you feel your emotions starting to escalate, take a deep breath and give yourself a moment to process what's happening. By pausing, you create the space needed to choose how you want to respond rather than reacting impulsively. A simple technique is to count to five before responding to a question or comment that triggers strong emotions.

2. **Shift from Reaction to Reflection**

   When faced with an emotional test, instead of reacting to her words or behavior, take a step back and **reflect** on the situation. Ask yourself questions like:

   o "What is she really asking me?"
   o "Why am I feeling triggered right now?"
   o "What kind of response will strengthen the relationship?"

   This shift from reaction to reflection helps you stay grounded and avoid saying or doing things you might regret later.

3. **Focus on the Bigger Picture**

   It's important to keep in mind that tests are often not personal attacks. They are opportunities for growth and understanding in the relationship. When you recognize that her behavior is not an attack on you, but rather an evaluation of your character and emotional stability, you can approach the situation with more calmness and clarity.

# The Importance of Self-Awareness and Understanding Emotional Triggers

**Self-awareness** is the foundation of emotional mastery. Understanding your emotions and recognizing what triggers them will help you manage your reactions more effectively. When you're self-aware, you can identify patterns in your emotional responses and take proactive steps to avoid negative reactions in the future.

## Here's why self-awareness matters:

1. **Recognizing Your Emotional Triggers**

   Everyone has emotional triggers—certain words, behaviors, or situations that provoke a strong emotional response. For example, if you've been hurt in the past by someone breaking promises, you might feel anger or frustration when your partner brings up an issue related to trust. By identifying these triggers, you can work on responding calmly rather than reacting impulsively. A good exercise is to write down common situations that upset you and reflect on why they trigger such strong emotions.

2. **Understanding the Root of Your Emotions**

   Emotions often come from deeper beliefs, fears, or past experiences. For instance, if you feel defensive when she asks about your future plans, it may be rooted in a fear of commitment or insecurity about your own direction in life. By exploring the root of your emotions, you can address these deeper issues, which will help you handle future emotional challenges more effectively.

### 3. Recognizing Emotional Patterns

Over time, you'll begin to notice patterns in how you react to certain situations. Perhaps when she asks for space, you feel neglected or insecure, even if there's no real cause for concern. Recognizing these patterns allows you to make intentional changes. Once you understand why you react the way you do, you can develop healthier emotional responses.

## Practical Exercises to Stay Calm and Composed in Moments of Tension

Now that you understand the importance of emotional mastery and self-awareness, let's discuss some practical exercises you can use to stay calm and composed when emotions run high.

### 1. Breathing Techniques

One of the simplest yet most effective ways to calm yourself in tense moments is by practicing deep breathing. When you feel your emotions rising, take a slow, deep breath in for four counts, hold it for four counts, and then exhale slowly for four counts. Repeat this for 1-2 minutes until you feel your body relax. This practice helps activate your body's relaxation response and creates space to think clearly before reacting.

### 2. Mindfulness and Grounding Exercises

Being present in the moment can help you avoid being overwhelmed by emotions. A mindfulness exercise you can try is the "5-4-3-2-1" grounding technique:

o **5** things you can see
o **4** things you can touch

- o **3** things you can hear
- o **2** things you can smell
- o **1** thing you can taste

This simple exercise focuses your attention on the present, distracting you from the emotions that might be running high. It helps ground you and brings your awareness back to the current moment.

### 3. Journaling to Process Emotions

After experiencing a challenging moment, take some time to reflect by writing down your thoughts and feelings in a journal. Journaling allows you to process your emotions and gain clarity on why you reacted the way you did. It can also help you identify patterns in your emotional responses, which will guide you in making more conscious choices in the future.

### 4. Visualization

Visualization is a powerful technique to help you stay calm and composed in stressful situations. Before you're faced with a potential emotional challenge, close your eyes and visualize yourself handling the situation with calmness and confidence. Imagine yourself responding with a clear, composed voice and staying true to your values, no matter the test. This mental rehearsal helps prepare you for real-life situations and strengthens your emotional resilience.

### 5. Physical Activity

Physical activity can also be a great way to release built-up tension and calm your mind. Whether it's going for a run, doing yoga, or practicing some light stretching, moving your body helps release stress and boosts your mood. Exercise is an excellent way to reset your emotions when you feel overwhelmed by a situation.

## Conclusion

Emotional mastery is a vital skill for handling the tests women give men. By controlling your emotional responses, understanding your emotional triggers, and practicing techniques to stay calm, you can navigate relationship challenges with confidence and composure. The ability to pause, reflect, and respond thoughtfully rather than impulsively will help you build stronger, more stable relationships. Remember, emotional mastery isn't about suppressing your emotions—it's about understanding them, managing them, and choosing the best way to respond in every situation. Through practice and self-awareness, you can become the emotionally intelligent partner that any woman would be proud to have by her side.

# Building Self Confidence

One of the most powerful qualities you can develop as a man is **self-confidence**. When you have a solid sense of who you are, what you stand for, and what you bring to the table, you can approach relationship challenges—including the tests women give—without feeling threatened or insecure. This chapter is about how you can build and nurture your self-confidence, so that when faced with her tests, you not only pass them but do so with ease and poise.

### Developing a Solid Sense of Self-Worth and Independence

At the core of self-confidence is **self-worth**—the belief that you are valuable, capable, and deserving of respect and love. This sense of self-worth forms the foundation of your emotional stability and helps you maintain your calm in the face of challenges. When you feel secure in who you are, you won't be easily rattled by the subtle or direct tests that women often use to assess your character and emotional strength.

Here's how you can develop a strong sense of self-worth:

1. **Know Your Value**

   Understand what makes you unique and what you bring to the relationship. This isn't about arrogance or pride; it's about recognizing your strengths and acknowledging your worth. Whether it's your work ethic, your kindness, your intelligence, or your sense of humor, knowing what you offer will prevent you from questioning yourself when faced with her tests. **Affirmations** can be a helpful tool here. Each day, repeat positive statements about yourself like, "I am worthy of love and respect," or "I bring valuable qualities to my relationships." This builds an inner belief that will stay with you when challenges arise.

2. **Cultivate Independence**

   A confident man is one who has his own life, passions, and goals. When you are independent—emotionally and physically—you don't rely on your partner to fill every need or define your sense of self-worth. You have your own passions, hobbies, and ambitions that make you feel fulfilled, regardless of her tests or opinions. By developing emotional independence, you also show her that you're not threatened by her independence or need for space. You are secure enough to give her the freedom to be herself, which only strengthens the relationship.

   Take time to focus on your own interests, whether it's working on a personal project, pursuing a hobby, or investing time in your health and well-being. When you feel confident in your own life and your ability to take care of yourself, you won't feel like her behavior is an attack on you. You'll see her tests as opportunities for growth, rather than threats to your stability.

3. **Set Healthy Boundaries**

Part of developing self-worth is learning to set healthy boundaries in relationships. This means understanding where your limits are and having the confidence to communicate those limits. When you are clear about your own values and priorities, you will not be swayed or manipulated by her behavior. Healthy boundaries show that you respect yourself, and they set the tone for a relationship based on mutual respect.

## Focusing on Your Passions, Purpose, and Personal Growth

Self-confidence grows when you are actively engaged in your own life and growth. When you are passionate about something, driven by a purpose, and committed to improving yourself, you naturally exude confidence. Your self-esteem doesn't hinge on how she reacts to you or whether you pass every test. Instead, it comes from knowing that you are growing into the best version of yourself, regardless of the challenges you face in your relationship.

Here's how you can nurture this kind of confidence:

1. **Pursue Your Passions**

Self-confidence flourishes when you spend time doing things that excite and fulfill you. Whether it's your career, a creative pursuit, fitness, or learning new skills, immersing yourself in activities you care about will give you a deep sense of accomplishment and pride.

When you're passionate about your life outside of the relationship, you bring a sense of purpose and enthusiasm into the relationship, too.

## 2. Stay Focused on Your Purpose

A man who knows his purpose in life is a man who carries himself with confidence. Your purpose could be related to your career, family, community involvement, or personal mission. When you have a strong sense of direction, you'll handle tests with clarity and confidence, because you know that you have something bigger than the relationship driving you. Women are drawn to men who are grounded in their purpose, because they bring a sense of stability and vision to the relationship.

To build this, spend time reflecting on your goals and values. Ask yourself, "What do I want to achieve in life? What am I working toward? What do I believe in?" Knowing the answers to these questions helps you stay anchored in your own sense of purpose, which will make you less susceptible to doubt or insecurity during moments of tension.

## 3. Commit to Personal Growth

Confidence isn't about being perfect—it's about continuously striving to improve. Men who are confident are often those who embrace self-growth and take responsibility for their own development. This could mean improving your communication skills, deepening your emotional intelligence, working on physical health, or learning to manage stress. The more you grow, the more you build a solid foundation of self-assurance.

Take small, consistent actions toward self-improvement. Whether it's reading books on personal development, setting goals for fitness, or finding mentors who inspire you, every step forward increases your confidence and sense of self-worth.

4. **Embrace the Challenge of Change**

Life and relationships constantly evolve, and confidence comes from knowing that you can adapt to change. When challenges arise—whether in your relationship or your personal life—view them as opportunities for growth rather than threats. Embrace change with a mindset of resilience and openness, knowing that each challenge you overcome adds to your confidence.

## Conclusion

Building self-confidence is a journey that requires self-awareness, commitment to personal growth, and a deep understanding of your own value. By developing a strong sense of self-worth and independence, you can approach any test with calmness and clarity, knowing that you are enough just as you are. When you focus on your passions, purpose, and continuous improvement, you'll exude confidence naturally, making you not only more attractive to women, but also more secure and fulfilled in your own life. Self-confidence is not something you can fake—it's something that grows from within, through consistent effort and self-reflection.

## Strong Communication Skills

One of the most important skills in any relationship is **strong communication**. Communication is the bridge that connects you and your partner, allowing both of you to understand each other's thoughts, emotions, and needs. When it comes to the tests that women give men, your ability to communicate clearly, honestly, and openly can make all the difference. This chapter will explore why communication is so essential, how to respond to tough questions and challenges with confidence, and how to do all of this with compassion and understanding.

## The Importance of Clear, Honest, and Open Communication

Effective communication is the foundation of trust, respect, and intimacy in a relationship. When you communicate clearly and honestly, you create an environment where both partners feel heard, understood, and valued. This is especially important when navigating the emotional tests that women often give men.

### 1. Clarity Brings Understanding

When you communicate in a way that is clear and straightforward, there is less room for confusion and misinterpretation. Women often test men by asking tough questions or presenting emotional challenges. If you respond with clarity, you show that you are confident and not afraid to address difficult topics. Clear communication helps avoid unnecessary misunderstandings, making it easier for both of you to feel secure and connected.

### 2. Honesty Builds Trust

Trust is the cornerstone of any relationship, and honesty is the key to building that trust. Women want to feel safe in a relationship, knowing that they can count on you to be truthful, even when the truth might be difficult to hear or admit. Honesty doesn't mean being brutally blunt, but it does mean being real and transparent. When you are honest in your communication, you show that you are trustworthy and reliable, which is exactly what women need in a partner.

3. **Openness Encourages Connection**

Openness is about being vulnerable and allowing your partner to see who you truly are. When you are open in your communication, you invite her to share her own thoughts, feelings, and needs, too. This creates a deeper emotional connection and helps both of you understand each other on a much more meaningful level. Women often test men to see how open and emotionally available they are. By being open in your communication, you demonstrate emotional maturity and readiness to be in a meaningful relationship.

## Answering Tough Questions and Challenges with Confidence and Compassion

In any relationship, difficult conversations and challenging questions will arise. When you face these tests, how you respond matters. The way you handle tough questions reflects your emotional maturity, confidence, and respect for your partner's needs. Responding with both **confidence** and **compassion** allows you to answer these challenges without hesitation, while also showing empathy and care for her feelings.

1. **Answering Tough Questions with Confidence**

When faced with a tough question, the best approach is to answer with confidence and composure. Hesitation or avoidance can create doubt and insecurity. If she asks you, "How serious are you about this relationship?" or "Where do you see this going?" take a moment to reflect on your answer, but speak clearly and decisively. A response such as, "I'm serious about building something meaningful with you," shows confidence and clarity.

When you answer confidently, it shows that you have thought about the relationship and are not afraid to express your intentions. Confidence doesn't mean having all the answers, but it does mean standing firm in your values and what you want for the future.

## 2. Compassionate Communication

While confidence is important, compassion is equally vital. Women want to feel heard and understood, especially during emotional moments. Even when answering difficult questions, it's essential to respond with **empathy** and **understanding**. If she asks something vulnerable, such as, "Do you still care about me?" your response should acknowledge her feelings, as well as provide reassurance. You might say, "I understand why you might feel uncertain, but I care deeply about you, and I want to continue building our relationship together."

Compassionate communication is not about avoiding tough topics, but about responding with kindness and understanding. It shows that you care not only about the answer you're giving but also about how she feels in the moment. A compassionate response helps her feel safe, secure, and emotionally connected to you.

## 3. Avoiding Defensive Responses

One common mistake men make when faced with difficult questions or challenges is becoming defensive. It's natural to feel like you're being attacked or tested, but getting defensive only escalates the situation and makes communication harder. Instead of immediately reacting with frustration or anger, pause and take a deep breath. Consider her question from her perspective, and answer thoughtfully.

For example, if she asks, "Why didn't you call me back earlier?" instead of responding with irritation, you could say, "I'm sorry for not getting back to you sooner. I was busy with work, but I understand how that might have upset you. Let's talk about it."

By avoiding defensiveness, you create space for productive, open, and respectful communication that addresses the issue, rather than making it worse.

4. **Active Listening**

Strong communication isn't just about what you say; it's also about how you listen. When your partner speaks, give her your full attention. This means putting down distractions like your phone or TV and focusing on her words, tone, and body language. Active listening shows that you respect her feelings and are invested in what she has to say. When you listen actively, you're more likely to respond with the right words, tone, and compassion.

In moments of testing, when she asks you a question or shares her concerns, listen carefully without interrupting or jumping to conclusions. By doing so, you'll show her that you value her thoughts and are willing to understand her perspective before responding.

## Conclusion

Clear, honest, and open communication is essential for navigating the emotional tests women give men. By answering tough questions with confidence and compassion, and by practicing active listening, you build trust, strengthen your emotional connection, and show emotional maturity. Communication is not just about conveying information—it's about creating an environment where both partners feel understood, valued, and emotionally safe. By mastering the art of communication, you'll be able to handle any test with ease and build a strong, lasting connection with your partner.

# Strengthening Masculinity and Leadership

In every relationship, strong masculinity and leadership play crucial roles. These qualities are not about dominance or control, but about having the ability to make decisions, take responsibility, and lead with calmness and confidence. Cultivating these traits will help you become the man who not only passes the tests women give but also becomes a true source of stability, direction, and emotional strength in the relationship. In this chapter, we'll explore how to strengthen your masculinity and leadership skills, both in your personal life and in your relationship.

## Cultivating Strong Decision-Making Skills, Responsibility, and a Sense of Direction

One of the hallmarks of strong masculinity is the ability to make decisions confidently. When you are decisive, it shows that you are in control of your life and capable of taking responsibility for your actions.

Women often look for men who can make decisions, especially when facing challenges or when the relationship requires clarity. Here's how to develop those skills:

1. **Developing Decision-Making Skills**

   Strong decision-making starts with being clear about your values, goals, and priorities. The more you know what you want in life, the easier it becomes to make choices that align with your true self. Whether you are making decisions about your career, relationships, or personal growth, staying connected to your core values helps you move forward with confidence.

   A simple way to improve your decision-making is to practice making small decisions regularly. For example, decide what to eat, what book to read, or what hobby you want to pursue. The more you practice, the more confident you will become in your ability to make bigger, more impactful decisions.

2. **Taking Responsibility for Your Actions**

   Leadership and masculinity also mean taking full responsibility for your life. When things go wrong, it's easy to blame external circumstances or other people. However, true leaders own their mistakes and learn from them. This doesn't mean blaming yourself unnecessarily, but rather acknowledging when things haven't gone as planned and figuring out how to improve.

Responsibility also extends to the people in your life. If you make a commitment to your partner, make sure to follow through. Being a responsible man means that your words and actions are aligned, and your partner can trust you to take care of what matters.

### 3. Building a Sense of Direction

A man who lacks direction is more likely to feel lost or unsure when facing challenges, including tests in relationships. Building a sense of direction means knowing where you are headed in life—whether it's related to your career, personal goals, or relationships. A clear sense of direction helps you navigate difficult situations with confidence because you always know your "why."

To develop a sense of direction, take time to set long-term goals and break them down into smaller, manageable steps. These goals should reflect your values, desires, and vision for your future. Whether it's building a successful career, growing a meaningful relationship, or improving your physical health, working towards something larger than yourself gives you a sense of purpose and drives your decisions.

## Being a Calm and Assertive Leader in Your Life and Relationship

Leadership isn't about being loud, domineering, or controlling. True leadership is calm, assertive, and rooted in self-assurance. It means leading by example and guiding others without forceful behavior. This quality is especially important in relationships, where emotional stability and clarity are needed to maintain harmony and respect. Here's how to be a calm and assertive leader in your own life and in your relationship:

### 1. Leading with Calmness

A strong leader stays calm under pressure. When faced with challenges—whether it's a test from your partner or a stressful situation in your personal life—the ability to stay composed and grounded makes all the difference. Staying calm allows you to assess the situation clearly and make decisions without letting emotions cloud your judgment.

To practice calmness, try techniques like deep breathing, meditation, or mindfulness. These practices help you center yourself and manage your emotional responses. In moments of stress or emotional tension, pause before reacting. When you respond calmly, you show that you are capable of handling any situation with grace and wisdom.

## 2. Being Assertive, Not Aggressive

Assertiveness means expressing your needs, opinions, and boundaries with confidence and respect. It's different from aggression, which is about forcing your will on others. Assertiveness allows you to stand up for what you believe in, communicate openly, and respect your partner's needs, all while maintaining a healthy balance in the relationship.

For example, if you need time for yourself, say so assertively: "I need some quiet time to recharge," instead of letting frustration build up. In relationships, assertiveness means being clear about your feelings, setting boundaries when necessary, and leading without creating conflict or tension.

## 3. Leading by Example

A great leader doesn't just give orders or demand respect—they earn it by demonstrating the values and behaviors they expect from others. If you want your partner to respect your time, show that you respect hers. If you want to create trust in the relationship, be trustworthy in your actions. Being a strong leader means holding yourself accountable and setting the standard for how you expect to be treated.

4. **Guiding with Compassion**

Leadership in a relationship also involves guiding with compassion. While you should be confident and assertive, you also need to be empathetic and understanding of your partner's needs and feelings. A great leader listens, supports, and encourages growth, both in themselves and in others. Being compassionate in your leadership allows you to lead in a way that builds connection, trust, and mutual respect.

## Conclusion

Strengthening your masculinity and leadership isn't about becoming perfect or having all the answers. It's about developing the ability to make confident decisions, take responsibility, and lead your life with a clear sense of direction. A calm and assertive leader not only handles challenges with composure but also guides others with compassion and integrity. By cultivating these qualities, you'll become the man who is not only able to pass her tests but also the man she can rely on, trust, and look to for strength and stability in the relationship.

## Building Emotional Intelligence

Emotional intelligence is one of the most important qualities a man can develop in any relationship. It goes beyond simply managing your own emotions; it's about understanding, responding to, and empathizing with the emotions of others. When you build emotional intelligence, you gain the ability to interpret your partner's needs, reactions, and feelings—without taking things personally. This ability allows you to stay calm, grounded, and connected, even during times of emotional tension or when you're faced with challenges in the relationship.

In this section, we will explore how you can develop emotional intelligence by fostering empathy, practicing patience, and giving your partner the space she needs—without feeling rejected or distant.

## Developing Empathy and Understanding

Empathy is the ability to put yourself in someone else's shoes and feel what they feel. In a relationship, this skill is essential. Women often express their needs or emotions indirectly, and the key to understanding them lies in your ability to recognize those emotional cues and respond appropriately.

1. **Interpreting Her Needs Without Taking Tests Personally**

   One of the most important aspects of building emotional intelligence is not taking things personally, especially when faced with emotional tests. When women test men, they are not necessarily attacking or challenging them directly; rather, they are assessing their partner's emotional maturity, stability, and ability to handle stress.

   When she expresses her feelings—whether through words, body language, or tone—try to focus on understanding the underlying need. For example, if she is distant or quiet, it might not be a sign of rejection. She might simply need some space to process her thoughts or emotions. By developing empathy, you can recognize when these are signals rather than tests, and approach them with patience instead of defensiveness.

   A great way to practice empathy is by listening without interrupting. When she shares something, try to focus on how she feels, not just what she's saying. If you're unsure of her emotional state, ask open-ended questions to gain more understanding. For example, "It seems like you're feeling a bit upset—would you like to

86

talk about it?" This approach allows you to connect with her emotions, without assuming or jumping to conclusions.

## 2. Understanding Her Emotional Needs

Women's emotional needs can sometimes seem complex or difficult to decipher, but with empathy, you'll begin to notice patterns in her behavior and reactions. Pay attention to the things she values most, the way she communicates, and the signals she gives off. Understanding her emotional needs requires emotional awareness and the ability to look beyond the surface.

By consistently tuning into her emotional state, you will be able to respond with care and thoughtfulness, making her feel heard, validated, and supported. For instance, if she seems overwhelmed by something, acknowledging her stress and offering a solution or simply lending a listening ear can go a long way in strengthening the relationship.

## Practicing Patience

Patience is another key element of emotional intelligence. Relationships are not always smooth, and emotions can be unpredictable. Sometimes, she may need time to process her feelings or deal with her own personal challenges. The ability to remain patient and understanding in these moments is a hallmark of emotional maturity.

## 1. Giving Space Without Feeling Rejected

Giving her space when she asks for it can be difficult, especially if you interpret her request as a sign of rejection. However, emotional intelligence means recognizing that needing space is a normal, healthy part of relationships. It's a way for her to recharge, gather

her thoughts, and return to the relationship with clarity and emotional balance.

When she asks for space, rather than taking it personally, understand that it's not a reflection of your value or the relationship. It's simply a need for emotional balance. Allow her the time she needs without guilt or insecurity creeping in. Use that time to focus on your own personal growth or passions, and trust that the space will benefit the relationship in the long run.

2. **Responding with Patience Instead of Impatience**

In emotionally charged situations, it's easy to become frustrated or anxious. When tensions rise, patience allows you to remain calm and composed, while rushing to fix things or express frustration can escalate the situation. Instead of reacting impulsively, take a moment to breathe and assess the situation before responding.

Practicing patience also involves recognizing when she needs time to articulate her feelings. Don't interrupt or rush her to "fix" her emotions. Sometimes, just being present and listening is the most helpful thing you can do. Over time, your patience will help build trust and deepen the emotional connection between you both.

### Balancing Emotional Support and Personal Boundaries

Emotional intelligence is not just about responding to your partner's needs; it's also about maintaining your own emotional health and boundaries. In any relationship, it's essential to support your partner while also taking care of yourself. This means knowing when to give her the emotional support she needs, while also knowing when to take a step back to avoid emotional burnout.

1. **Setting Healthy Emotional Boundaries**

   Setting emotional boundaries doesn't mean being cold or distant—it means protecting your emotional well-being so you can show up as the best version of yourself for your partner. If her emotional state becomes overwhelming, it's okay to express that you need some time to process the situation, too. By doing so, you demonstrate emotional maturity and self-awareness.

   Healthy boundaries also mean not absorbing her emotions or letting her emotional tests take over your sense of self. You can empathize and offer support without letting her emotions dictate how you feel or react. This balance ensures that you can remain emotionally stable while still being there for her when she needs you most.

---

## Conclusion

Building emotional intelligence is about understanding yourself and your partner on a deeper level. It's about developing the ability to recognize emotional cues, interpret them without judgment, and respond with empathy and patience. When you cultivate emotional intelligence, you become more attuned to her needs, less reactive to emotional tests, and more equipped to handle challenges with grace.

By embracing empathy, practicing patience, and maintaining emotional balance, you create a safe and supportive environment where both you and your partner can grow together. Emotional intelligence is a lifelong skill that, when nurtured, leads to deeper connection, stronger communication, and a more fulfilling relationship.

# The Power of integrity and Authenticity

Integrity and authenticity are two of the most powerful traits a man can embody in a relationship. They form the foundation of trust, respect, and genuine connection. When you stay true to your values, regardless of the pressure you might feel, you become a man who naturally passes her tests without even trying. Authenticity allows you to be your true self, creating a strong, lasting bond with your partner. In this chapter, we'll explore why embracing your values and staying authentic is so important in relationships and how it makes navigating tests easier.

## Embracing Your Values

Your values are the principles that guide your actions, decisions, and interactions. They define who you are and what you stand for. Integrity is about consistently aligning your actions with these values, even when faced with challenges or pressure. When you act with integrity, you demonstrate that you are a man of character, someone who can be trusted and relied upon.

1. **Staying True to Your Values Under Pressure**

    Life, especially in relationships, often tests us in ways that challenge our core beliefs. It might be a moment where you're asked to compromise your values for the sake of avoiding conflict, or maybe you're tempted to take the easier route. However, true integrity means standing firm in what you believe, even when it's difficult or uncomfortable.

    For example, if you value honesty, there may be times when telling the truth feels risky, especially if it could upset your partner or create tension. But integrity means you speak your truth with kindness and respect, knowing that long-term trust is built on transparency. When you remain steadfast in your values, you earn your partner's respect and strengthen the emotional connection between you both.

2. **The Power of Consistency**

When your actions consistently reflect your values, you create a sense of security and stability in the relationship. Your partner knows that they can trust you to act with honesty, loyalty, and respect, regardless of the situation. This consistency is crucial in passing any test, as it reassures your partner that you're dependable, genuine, and emotionally grounded.

## Authenticity Makes Tests Easier

Authenticity is about being true to yourself. It means not pretending to be someone you're not, and it's one of the most attractive qualities you can possess in a relationship. When you're authentic, you don't have to worry about keeping up appearances or figuring out which version of yourself to show. Instead, you can be genuine and confident in who you are, making it easier to navigate the natural challenges and tests that come your way.

1. **Being Yourself Without Pretense**

One of the biggest mistakes men make is trying to be someone they're not in order to impress or gain approval. Whether it's pretending to like certain things, exaggerating accomplishments, or pretending to be more confident than you really feel, all of these actions create unnecessary pressure and can lead to insecurity and stress.

When you embrace authenticity, you remove the need for these pretenses. You allow yourself to be vulnerable, showing your true self with all its strengths and flaws. This doesn't mean being perfect—it means being honest about who you are, what you believe, and what you need. Authenticity makes passing her tests easier because you don't have to guess what she wants or try to conform to her expectations. You simply show up as yourself, and that's enough.

## 2. How Authenticity Eases Relationship Challenges

Tests in relationships can be challenging, but when you approach them with authenticity, the process becomes more natural. For example, if your partner is testing your emotional stability or your leadership qualities, being authentic means you don't need to pretend to have all the answers or appear completely in control. You simply acknowledge the situation, express how you feel, and respond in a way that aligns with your true self.

When you act authentically, you demonstrate emotional intelligence and self-awareness, qualities that naturally help you navigate tests with ease. You become more confident in your responses because you're not trying to play a role or meet external expectations—you're simply showing up as who you are.

## The Link Between Integrity, Authenticity, and Relationship Success

Integrity and authenticity work hand in hand. When you embrace both, you create a powerful foundation for a healthy, long-lasting relationship. Integrity ensures that your actions reflect your true values, while authenticity allows you to show your partner who you really are. Together, these qualities make passing her tests not only easier but also more meaningful.

By consistently aligning with your values and staying true to yourself, you establish trust and emotional security in the relationship. Your partner will appreciate your honesty and reliability, and the emotional bond between you both will deepen.

When you stop trying to impress or please her with false versions of yourself, the relationship becomes more genuine, making it easier to face challenges and grow together.

---

## Conclusion

Embracing integrity and authenticity transforms not only how you handle tests but also the entire dynamic of your relationship. When you stay true to your values and remain authentic in your actions and words, you create a solid foundation of trust and respect. This natural approach to relationships allows you to pass tests with ease, without the stress of pretending or second-guessing yourself.

Remember, the best version of you is the one that is true to yourself. Authenticity and integrity will always lead to a deeper, more meaningful connection, and they will help you navigate the ups and downs of any relationship with grace and confidence.

---

# 5

# My Personal Story

As I reflect on my own experiences navigating relationships, I can't help but acknowledge the role these subtle "tests" played in shaping who I am today. Early on, like many men, I didn't fully understand what was happening when I encountered these challenges. In fact, I often misinterpreted them as personal attacks or as attempts to undermine me. But with time, patience, and self-awareness, I began to realize that these were opportunities for growth - both for me as a man and for the relationship as a whole.

One of the first tests I remember clearly was an emotional stability test. It happened during a moment of stress in my relationship when I was dealing with a difficult situation at work. My partner, noticing I was a bit distant and distracted, asked me, "How do you handle stress? What happens when things go wrong?" At the time, I was overwhelmed and didn't recognize it as a test. I responded defensively, brushing it off with a vague, "I'll figure it out."

I could tell that something was off. The atmosphere felt tense, and I realized later that I had missed an important opportunity to show emotional maturity. My failure to remain calm and composed created distance between us. I had allowed stress to dictate my behavior, instead of using it as a chance to demonstrate my ability to handle pressure. Looking back, I see now that she wasn't questioning my abilities as much as she was gauging my emotional stability.

This was a turning point for me. Instead of reacting in frustration, I learned to approach these types of situations with a calm, solution-oriented mindset. I realized that being open about my emotions—

acknowledging the stress but showing my determination to overcome it—would have been the stronger, more connected response.

Then there was the time she asked me, "Where do you see this relationship going?" At that moment, I froze. I wasn't sure where I saw things going. I had been unsure about commitment, and I avoided the conversation by offering a non-committal answer, "I'm not sure yet."

That answer didn't sit well with her. I could sense that my vagueness caused her to feel uncertain about where we stood. She wanted clarity and assurance, and I had failed to provide that. I realized that avoiding tough conversations like this only created more distance, not less. The next time a similar question came up, I didn't hesitate. I shared my thoughts honestly, expressed my intentions clearly, and showed her that I was committed to building something serious. This level of transparency and sincerity not only helped us grow closer but also proved to both of us that we were on the same page.

There were also times when I was tested in ways I didn't expect. I remember once when she asked, "How would you feel if I needed some space?" Initially, I felt a twinge of insecurity. In the past, I might have reacted with jealousy or clinginess, unsure if she needed space because of something I had done wrong. But I learned that this wasn't about me—it was about her need for personal time to recharge.

Rather than feeling rejected, I responded with understanding, "I think it's healthy for us to have our own time. I want you to feel comfortable and supported." This response didn't just show my emotional maturity—it demonstrated respect for her autonomy, which is key to maintaining a healthy relationship.

What I've come to realize through these experiences is that these tests were never meant to trip me up or cause conflict. Instead, they were opportunities for me to show up as a better, stronger version of myself. The key was learning to recognize the tests for what they were and responding with integrity, calmness, and authenticity.

Each time I passed a test—or failed and learned from it—the relationship deepened. I stopped trying to "pass" the test just to gain approval. Instead, I began responding to these moments with authenticity, staying true to myself and my values. And that made all the difference.

As I share these personal experiences, my hope is that you, too, will come to see these tests not as obstacles but as opportunities to grow. Embrace them as moments to demonstrate who you really are. By doing so, you will not only pass the tests but also build a deeper connection with the woman in your life.

# Conclusion

As we've explored throughout this book, the tests women give men are not obstacles to fear, but opportunities for growth and deeper connection. These tests often come in subtle forms, and many men, myself included, can miss or misinterpret them in the heat of the moment. But the key to passing these tests isn't about playing a role or trying to impress—it's about being genuine, emotionally stable, and aligned with your values.

In my own journey, I learned that these tests are not about proving something to her, but about showing up as the best version of yourself. Whether it's showing emotional maturity under stress, being clear about your intentions for the future, or demonstrating respect for her autonomy, each test offers a chance to build trust, strengthen your bond, and reinforce your masculinity and leadership.

As I reflect on the times when I failed these tests, I see them now as stepping stones that helped me become a better partner and a more self-assured man. Each challenge was an opportunity to learn about myself, to practice emotional mastery, and to communicate more clearly and authentically. These moments taught me that growth doesn't happen in the absence of challenges—it happens through them.

The tests women give are not about manipulating or trapping you. They are, in fact, an invitation to rise to the occasion, to understand her needs and to become the man who can meet them with confidence and compassion. By embracing these moments, you not only become stronger but also more attuned to your partner, creating a deeper, more meaningful connection.

Ultimately, the key to passing any test lies in how you show up. Be calm, be authentic, and most importantly, be true to yourself. When you embrace these principles, you'll find that the tests become easier to navigate, and your relationship will grow stronger with each challenge faced together.

Remember, the journey is about progress, not perfection. Take the lessons you've learned from these tests and use them to build the kind of relationship that is rooted in trust, respect, and genuine love. When you do, you'll realize that passing these tests was never really the goal—the true goal is creating a partnership where both of you can thrive and grow together.

# References

Listed below are a number of references used to write this book as well as my personal experience.

1. **Gray, J.** (1992). *Men Are from Mars, Women Are from Venus.* HarperCollins.

   This classic book explores the differences in how men and women communicate, providing insight into the dynamics of relationships and how to understand the opposite sex.

2. **Gottman, J., & Silver, N.** (1999). *The Seven Principles for Making Marriage Work.* Three Rivers Press.

   A deep dive into the key principles that contribute to a healthy and lasting relationship, offering valuable lessons on emotional intelligence, communication, and conflict resolution.

3. **Tannen, D.** (1990). *You Just Don't Understand: Women and Men in Conversation.* Ballantine Books.

   This book examines how communication styles differ between men and women, shedding light on the subtle and often subconscious "tests" that women may give men.

4. **DeAngelis, T.** (2017). *Emotional Intelligence: Why It Can Matter More Than IQ.* Pearson Education.

This resource delves into emotional intelligence and its impact on relationships, providing a framework for understanding emotional responses and building stronger interpersonal connections.

5. **Dutton, D. G., & White, K. A.** (2013). *The Male Brain.* HarperCollins.
   Offers insights into the psychology of men, explaining how men react to emotional triggers and the importance of emotional mastery in relationships.

6. **Barker, G.** (2005). *Diversity and Masculinities.* Polity Press.
   Explores the concept of masculinity from multiple perspectives, emphasizing how men can develop healthier, more authentic forms of masculinity that benefit both themselves and their relationships.

7. **Parker-Pope, T.** (2010). *For Better: How the Surprising Science of Happy Couples Can Help Your Marriage Succeed.* HarperCollins.

   This book reveals findings from relationship science, offering strategies for strengthening partnerships and better understanding the dynamics that lead to long-term success.

8. **Schwartz, S. H.** (2012). *The Schwartz Value Survey.*
   A scholarly reference discussing values and how they influence behavior in relationships, particularly focusing on integrity and personal growth.

9. **Miller, J. B.** (1986). *The Development of Women's Sense of Self.* Harvard University Press.

Explores the psychological and emotional development of women, particularly their needs for security, trust, and emotional stability in relationships.

10. **Sternberg, R. J.** (1986). *The Triangle of Love: Intimacy, Passion, Commitment.* The Journal of Social and Personal Relationships. This article presents a theoretical framework of love and relationships, highlighting the importance of emotional stability, commitment, and mutual understanding.

These references provide a foundation for understanding the dynamics of relationships, emotional intelligence, and the nuances of male-female communication, all of which are essential for navigating the tests women give men.